MUSICAL INSTRUMENTS OF THE WORLD

Percussion

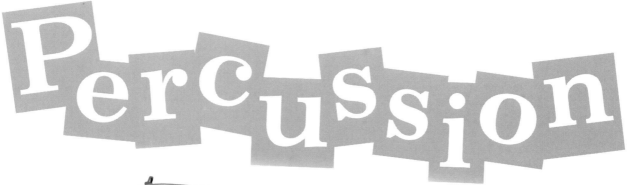

Barrie Carson Turner

Illustrated by John See

Smart Apple Media

First published in the UK in 1998 by
Belitha Press Limited
London House, Great Eastern Wharf,
Parkgate Road, London SW11 4NQ

Text by Barrie Carson Turner   Illustrations by John See
Text and illustrations copyright © Belitha Press Ltd 1998
Cover design by The Design Lab

Published in the United States by
Smart Apple Media
123 South Broad Street
Mankato, Minnesota 56001

ISBN: 1-887068-46-5

Library of Congress Cataloging-in-Publication Data

Turner, Barrie.
   Percussion / Barrie Carson Turner.
         p.   cm. — (The musical instruments of the world)
   Includes index.
   Summary: Describes nineteen percussion instruments from around the
world including the timpani, glockenspiel, claves, and talking drums.
   ISBN 1-887068-46-5
   1. Percussion instruments—Juvenile literature.   [1. Percussion
instruments.] I. Title. II. Series.
ML1030.T87 1998
786.8' 19—dc21   98-6278

Printed in Hong Kong / China

9   8   7   6   5   4   3

Picture acknowledgements: Axiom Photographic Agency: 27 James Morris;
The Hutchison Library: 4-5 Liba Taylor; Impact Photos: 22 Bruce Stephens;
Panos Pictures: 9 David Reed, 10-11 Guy Mansfield, 16-17 Sean Sprague;
Performing Arts Library: 13 Fritz Curzon, 14, 16 Clive Barda, 20-21 Steve Gillett,
28-29 Jane Mont Mitchell; Redferns: 6, 7, 12, 23, 26 Odile Noel, 8 Brigitte Engl,
24-25 David Redfern; Travel Link: 15 Brenda Kean; John Walmsley: 19.

Contents

Musical

Musical instruments are played in every country of the world. There are many thousands of different instruments in all shapes and sizes. They are often grouped into four families: strings, brass, percussion, and woodwind.

Percussion instruments are struck (hit), shaken, or scraped to make their sound. Brass and woodwind instruments are blown to make their sound. Stringed instruments sound when their strings vibrate.

instruments

This book is about the percussion family. Some of the instruments are quite unusual, and they certainly make some interesting sounds. Here you will find crashing cymbals, booming gongs, clicking castanets, talking drums, and jingling tambourines.

We have chosen 19 percussion instruments from around the world for this book. There is a picture of each instrument and a photograph of a performer playing it. On pages 30 and 31 you will find a list of useful words to help you understand more about music.

Timpani

Timpani are large drums that are part of an orchestra. Most orchestras have three or four. The timpani player (called a timpanist) presses a pedal at the bottom of the drum to change the pitch (make the notes higher or lower). The top of the drum is called the head or the skin. The body is called the bowl. Timpani are also called kettledrums.

Timpanists strike the top of the drums with drumsticks. Some drumsticks have soft felt ends; others have hard wooden ends.

head   bowl   drumsticks

pedal

6

Xylophone

The wooden notes of a xylophone (zy-low-fone) are called bars. They rest on pads or cords so that they ring clearly when struck. Small xylophones have a hollow wooden box underneath, others have a tube hanging below each bar. The box and tubes make the sound louder.

metal tubes (resonators)

bars

beaters

The xylophone is played with wooden sticks called beaters. Each beater has a round plastic or rubber head.

7

Gong

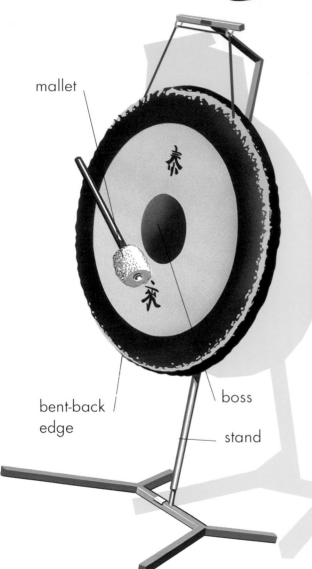

mallet

bent-back
edge

boss

stand

The gong is made from a large metal plate. In the middle there is a raised part called the boss. When this is struck, the gong makes its best sound. This instrument is so big it hangs on a stand. A gong is played with a wooden stick called a mallet, which has a soft felt head.

When the gong is struck hard it makes a loud booming sound that lasts a long time. Struck softly, it sounds mysterious.

Sansa

The sansa is from Africa. Its base is made from a wooden board or box, or a gourd (a pear-shaped fruit). On the top of the sansa, thin strips of iron are held in place by iron rods. Each strip sounds a different note. The long strips make the lowest sounds. The shorter strips make higher sounds.

iron tongue

board

iron rod

The player holds the sansa in both hands while he plucks the iron strips with his thumbs. The sansa is also called the mbira, or thumb piano.

9

Steel drums

Steel drums were invented about 60 years ago by Caribbean islanders. They discovered that the tops of large oil drums can make musical notes. Steel drums are played in sets.

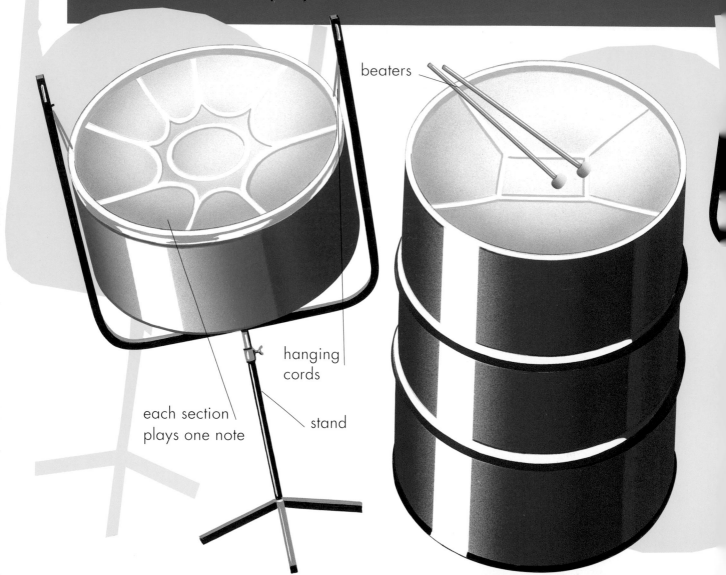

beaters

hanging cords

each section plays one note

stand

Players hit the top of the drums with short sticks called beaters. They have a bright, tinny tone and sound almost like bells.

The largest drums play low notes. The highest-sounding drum, which plays the tune, is called the ping-pong. To make steel drums, drum makers first saw off the bottom of an oil drum. Then the top is beaten into a saucer shape. Next, the drum maker divides the top into sections by making deep grooves in the metal. He or she taps and shapes each section until it sounds the correct note.

Cymbals

Cymbals have been played for thousands of years. Cymbals are thin and round, with a raised area in the middle. They have been made from many kinds of metal, even from gold. The tiniest cymbals are less than two inches across and are played between the fingers.

bronze metal

leather holding strap

raised area

Players hold a cymbal in each hand. They can clash them together loudly or rub them together quietly.

Scraper

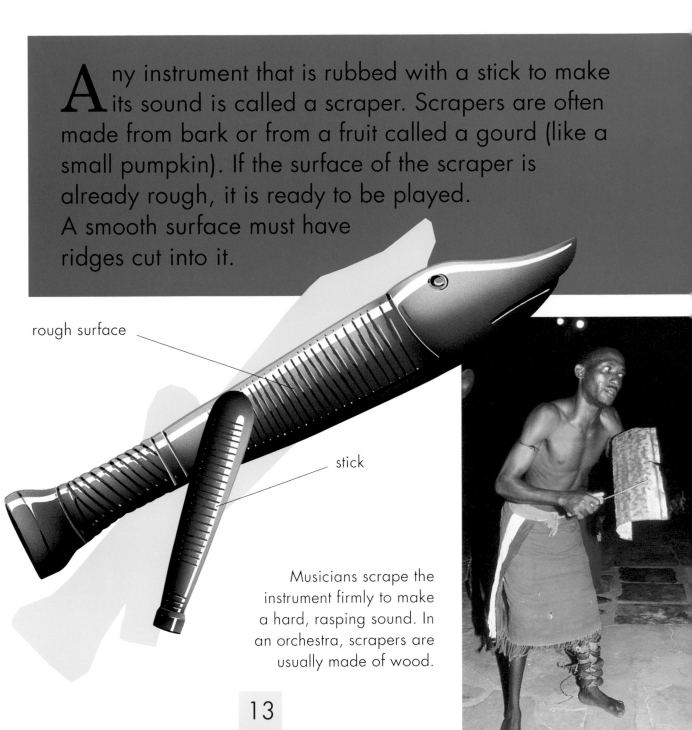

Any instrument that is rubbed with a stick to make its sound is called a scraper. Scrapers are often made from bark or from a fruit called a gourd (like a small pumpkin). If the surface of the scraper is already rough, it is ready to be played. A smooth surface must have ridges cut into it.

rough surface

stick

Musicians scrape the instrument firmly to make a hard, rasping sound. In an orchestra, scrapers are usually made of wood.

Glockenspiel

The glockenspiel (glock-en-shpeel) has metal notes called bars. It is played with two beaters that have round, hard ends. In an orchestra, the instrument rests on a table or on a stand. In marching bands, glockenspiels are turned upright so the notes face the player. *Glockenspiel* is a German word meaning "play of bells."

Players strike the bars in the middle to make the best sound. The sound of the glockenspiel is high, like a bell.

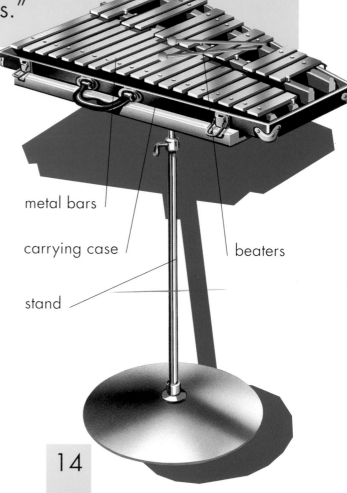

metal bars

carrying case

stand

beaters

14

Castanets

Castanets are played in pairs. They are held in the hand and clicked together. These instruments are wooden and shaped like a shell. They are hollowed out in the center, which makes the click sound louder. In Spain, dancers hold a pair of castanets in each hand, clicking them to keep time to dance movements.

hollowed-out center

thick cord

Dancers hold castanets by looping a cord around the thumb. Dancers hold smaller, higher-sounding castanets in the right hand and larger, lower-sounding ones in the left hand.

Marimba

The marimba comes from Africa, where the instrument is very popular in many areas. It has wooden notes, called bars, and is played with two sticks called beaters. If you play the notes from left to right, the sounds become higher as the bars get smaller.

The marimba is played in many parts of the world. Some very large marimbas are played by several musicians at once.

6

Large marimbas rest on a stand. Smaller ones hang around the player's neck. Some marimbas have hollowed-out gourds beneath the notes. The gourds make the sound louder and more rounded. In an orchestra, a marimba looks like a large xylophone, but a marimba's notes are lower.

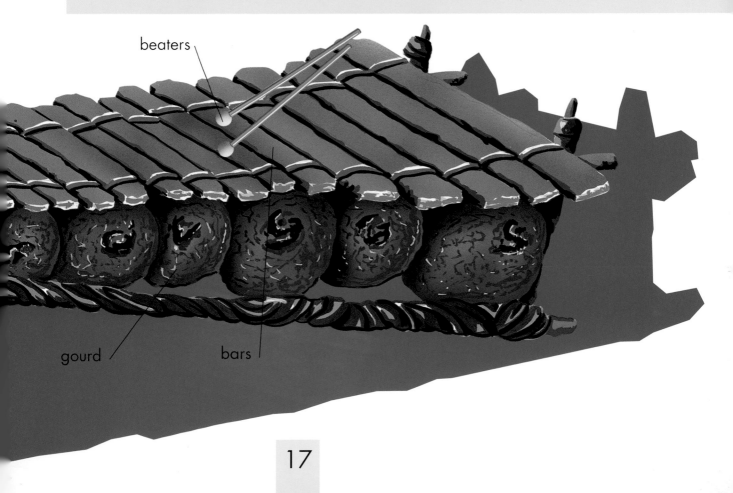

beaters

gourd

bars

Tubular bells

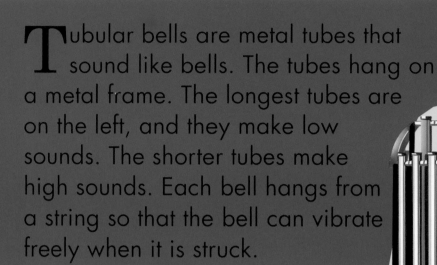

Tubular bells are metal tubes that sound like bells. The tubes hang on a metal frame. The longest tubes are on the left, and they make low sounds. The shorter tubes make high sounds. Each bell hangs from a string so that the bell can vibrate freely when it is struck.

mallet

The player taps the tubes near the top with a small wooden hammer called a mallet.

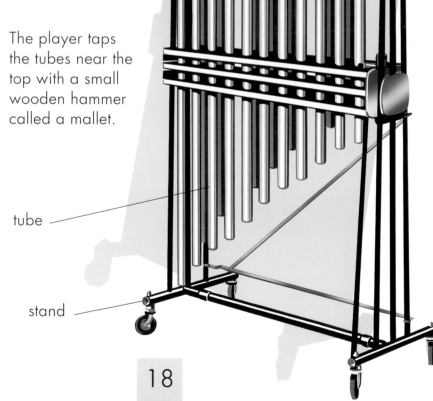

tube

stand

18

Claves

smooth
surface

Claves are two solid, tube-shaped sticks. The sticks are made from hard, smooth wood so that they make a bright, crisp click. Claves are also called percussion sticks. They were first played in Cuba. They are often used in South American dance music. Claves tap out important rhythms and help keep the beat.

rounded stick

The player holds one of the claves lightly in the palm of one hand and taps them together.

Rattles

Rattles have been played for thousands of years. These instruments are played in many types of music around the world. *Maracas* are hollow wooden rattles with pellets inside and are often used in South American dance music.

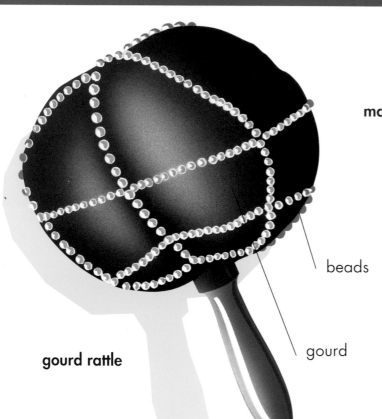

maracas

hollow wooden body

gourd rattle

beads

gourd

sleigh bells

bell

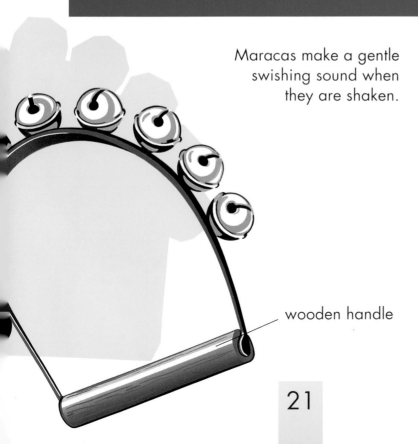

Sleigh bells are another kind of rattle. They are tiny metal bells tied to a strap or stick. Their jingly sound reminds many people of winter holidays. The gourd rattle is made from a pear-shaped fruit called a gourd. The fruit is dried until the seeds inside rattle when it is shaken. Sometimes the gourd is hollowed out and filled with other objects such as stones or small shells.

Maracas make a gentle swishing sound when they are shaken.

wooden handle

21

Tambourine

The tambourine looks like a small drum with small metal discs cut into the side. The discs are called jingles and look like tiny cymbals. When a player taps the tambourine, the discs sound like little bells. The top of the tambourine is called the skin, and the wooden side is called the frame.

skin

Players hold the tambourine in one hand and strike it with the other. Sometimes they shake it in the air.

frame

jingles

22

Tabla

The tabla is the name given to two drums from India. They often accompany a stringed instrument called the sitar. The top of the drum is called the head or skin. In the center of each skin, players smear a special black paste. This is called tuning paste, and it helps to make the sound clear and crisp. The drums rest on the floor on thick padded rings.

tuning paste

skin

Drummers sit cross-legged on the floor. They play using their fingertips and wrists. The larger drum makes the lower sounds.

23

Drum kit

The drum kit is most often played in rock, pop, and jazz music. The bass drum is the biggest and lowest-sounding drum. The next-largest drum is the tenor, which stands on legs. Two tom-toms are held on a stand above. The snare drum has wires along the bottom and makes a rattling sound when struck.

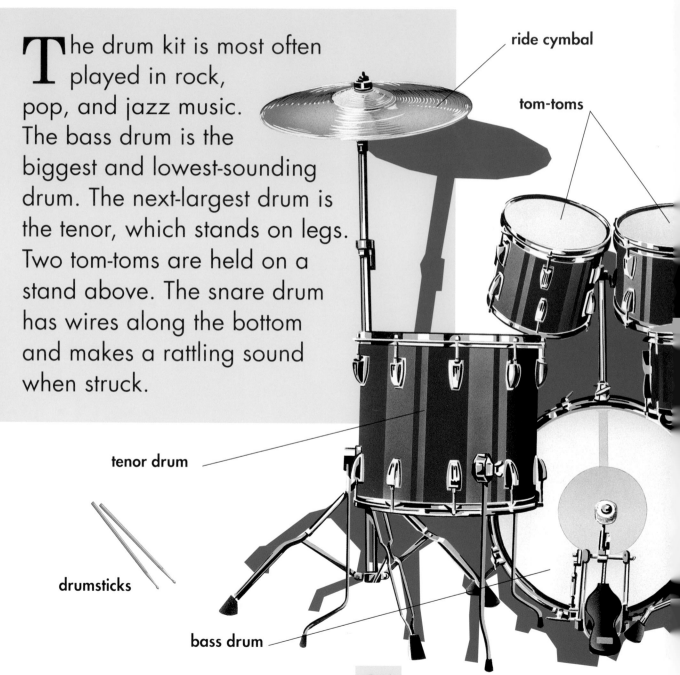

ride cymbal

tom-toms

tenor drum

drumsticks

bass drum

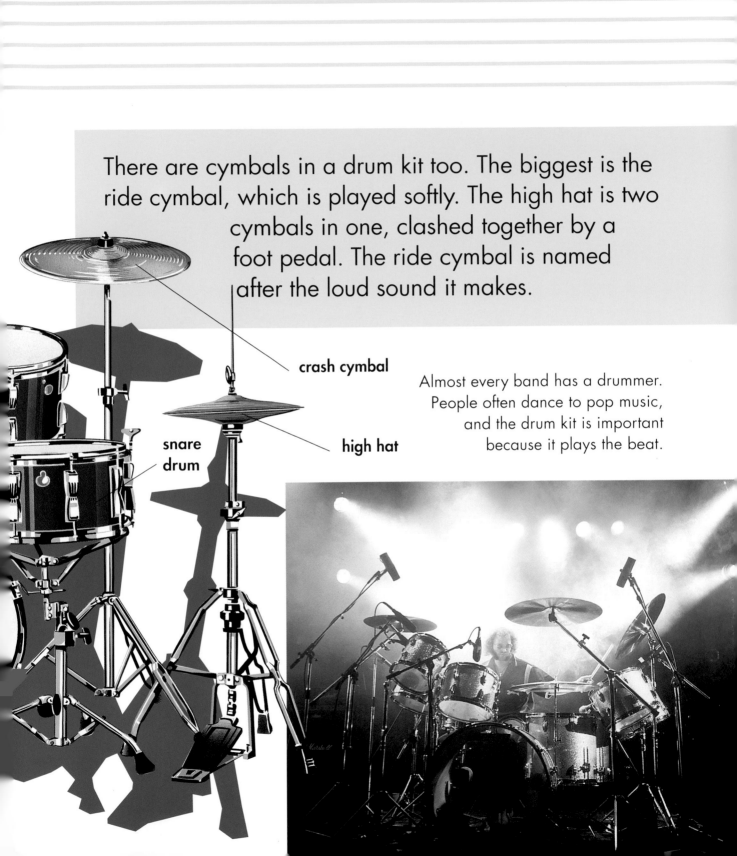

There are cymbals in a drum kit too. The biggest is the ride cymbal, which is played softly. The high hat is two cymbals in one, clashed together by a foot pedal. The ride cymbal is named after the loud sound it makes.

crash cymbal

snare drum

high hat

Almost every band has a drummer. People often dance to pop music, and the drum kit is important because it plays the beat.

Triangle

The triangle is an ancient instrument. It is made from a thin steel bar bent into the shape of a triangle with one corner left open. A triangle is held by a leather strap or string. Sometimes a triangle hangs from a music stand. The instrument is played with a short metal rod called a beater and makes a high tinkling sound.

If a player taps the triangle, it makes a quiet sound. For loud sounds, the beater is moved quickly from side to side.

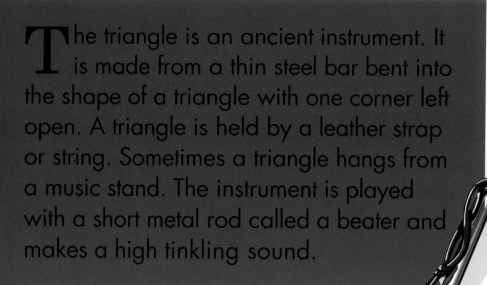

beater

holding strap

thin steel bar

Talking drum

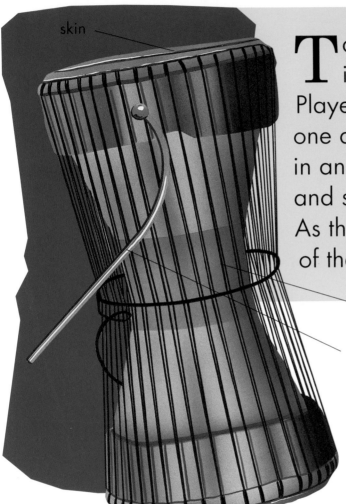

skin

string

drumstick

Talking drums are played in many parts of Africa. Players hold the drum under one arm and squeeze the sides in and out. This pulls on the strings and stretches the skin at the top. As the skin gets tighter, the pitch of the drum becomes higher.

Musicians play the drums using a curved wooden drumstick. The drum beats sound higher or lower, like a human voice, as the player squeezes the drum.

Bonang

The bonang is not one instrument, but several. It is a set of gongs and comes from Indonesia. Each gong is polished and shaped like a cooking pot with deep sides. The high raised area in the center is called the boss. Striking the boss makes the best sound.

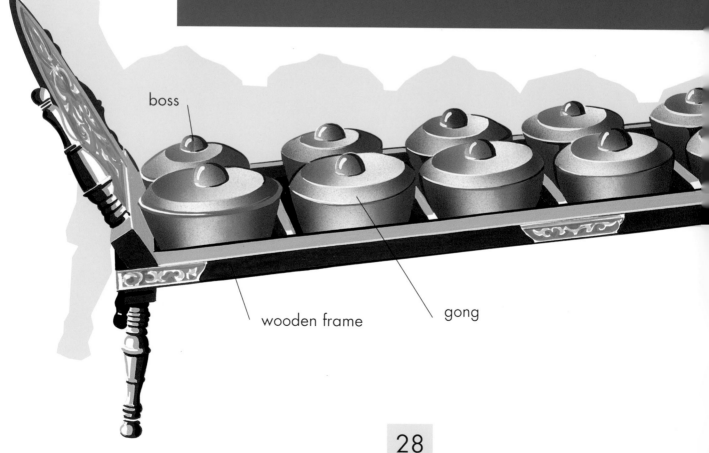

boss

wooden frame

gong

The gongs rest on cords so that they can vibrate freely. The cords are fastened to a carved wooden frame. Each gong sounds a different note. The bonang is played in the gamelan orchestra. It is used to accompany the tune.

Musicians strike the gongs with soft-ended sticks called beaters. The gongs make a soft bell-like sound.

Words to

bars The notes on some percussion instruments, such as the xylophone. The bars are struck with beaters to make the sound.

beat The steady pulse of the music.

beaters Sticks of wood or wire used to hit some instruments. The ends may be made of felt, rubber, or plastic.

boss The raised area in the center of a gong.

bowl The round, deep body of a drum.

cord A thin piece of rope or twisted pieces of string or silk.

family (of instruments) Instruments that are similar to each other.

frame A narrow band of wood on a small drum. The skin is stretched over the frame.

gamelan orchestra An orchestra from Indonesia that is made up of many different instruments.

head The part of a drum that is struck. It is also called the skin.

jazz A kind of pop music. In jazz, musicians often make up the music as they play it.

mallet A tiny wooden hammer used to play some instruments. It usually has a soft felt head.

marching band A group of musicians who play military (soldiers') music as they march along.

musician Someone who plays an instrument or sings.

music stand A frame that holds music so that a musician can see the music and play at the same time.

remember

oil drum A large, round metal container in which oil is stored.

orchestra A large group of musicians playing together.

pedal Any part of an instrument worked by the foot.

pellets Tiny balls of metal or other material inside a rattle.

performer Someone who plays or sings to other people.

pitch How high or low a sound is.

rattle An instrument that is shaken to make its sound.

resonator A tube, box, or gourd placed below the notes on a xylophone or marimba. They make the sound of the instrument louder and warmer.

rhythm A rhythm is made by the beat of the music and by how long and short the notes are.

rock A type of pop music that often has a strong beat.

scraper Any instrument that is scraped to make its sound.

sets Different sizes of the same instrument.

sitar One of the most important stringed instruments in India.

skin The part of a drum that is struck. It is also called the head.

strike To play an instrument by hitting it.

vibrate To move up and down very quickly. When a drum head is struck, it vibrates.

Index